Scorpio Horoscope 2025

By

Thalia C. Astraea

Table of Contents
<u>Scorpio (Oct. 23 – Nov. 21)</u>

Personality

Scorpio (October 23 – November 21), a Water sign ruled by Pluto and Mars, symbolizes intensity, transformation, and mystery. Represented by the Scorpion, Scorpios are known for their passionate, determined, and resourceful nature. They possess a depth of emotion and a keen intuition that allows them to navigate life's complexities with strength and resilience.

Core Traits of Scorpio

1. **Intense and Passionate:** Scorpios approach life with fervor, investing deeply in their goals, relationships, and interests.
2. **Mysterious and Enigmatic:** They often keep their true thoughts and feelings guarded, adding to their aura of intrigue.
3. **Determined and Resilient:** When Scorpios set their minds to something, they are unstoppable. They possess the inner strength to overcome challenges and emerge stronger.
4. **Resourceful and Strategic:** Scorpios excel at solving problems and finding creative solutions, even in difficult situations.

5. **Emotionally Intuitive:** Their strong intuition and emotional intelligence make them deeply empathetic and perceptive.

Strengths of Scorpio

- **Passion:** Scorpios bring energy and commitment to everything they do, making them powerful achievers and devoted partners.
- **Loyalty:** They are fiercely loyal to those they care about, standing by their loved ones through thick and thin.
- **Focus:** Scorpios can stay concentrated on their goals, often achieving remarkable success.
- **Emotional Depth:** They form deep connections and understand emotions on a profound level.
- **Transformative Power:** Scorpios thrive on growth and change, constantly evolving to become their best selves.

Weaknesses of Scorpio

- **Secretiveness:** Their guarded nature can sometimes make them appear distant or unapproachable.
- **Intensity:** Their emotional depth may feel overwhelming to others, and they can struggle with jealousy or possessiveness.

- **Stubbornness:** Scorpios may resist change or alternate viewpoints if they believe they are right.
- **Vengefulness:** When wronged, Scorpios may have difficulty letting go of grudges or seeking closure.
- **Control Issues:** Their desire to be in control can sometimes lead to tension in relationships or collaborations.

Scorpio in Relationships

As Partners:

Scorpios are deeply committed and passionate in relationships. They seek partners who can match their emotional depth and value loyalty and trust above all else.

- **Strengths in Love:** Devoted, passionate, and emotionally invested.
- **Challenges in Love:** Their intensity may feel overwhelming to some, and their guarded nature can create misunderstandings.

As Friends:

Scorpios are loyal and protective friends who value meaningful connections over superficial interactions. They are excellent confidants, offering support and wisdom.

- **Strengths in Friendship:** Loyal, empathetic, and reliable.
- **Challenges in Friendship:** They may struggle with opening up or forgiving easily when hurt.

As Family Members:

Scorpios bring emotional depth and unwavering support to family relationships. They are protective of their loved ones and value strong family bonds.

Scorpio in Career and Professional Life

Scorpios thrive in careers that require focus, strategy, and determination. They excel in roles that allow them to solve problems, explore mysteries, or make meaningful contributions.

Ideal Career Paths:

- **Psychology or Counseling:** Scorpios' emotional depth and intuition make them excellent at understanding and helping others.
- **Research or Science:** Their investigative nature is well-suited for roles requiring analysis and discovery.
- **Leadership or Management:** Scorpios excel in positions of power, where their determination and strategic thinking shine.

- **Arts or Writing:** Their creativity and passion translate well into storytelling, music, or visual arts.
- **Investigation or Law:** Careers in law enforcement, detective work, or legal professions align with their ability to uncover truths.

Workplace Traits:

- **Strengths:** Focused, resourceful, and innovative team members who excel in solving problems and leading projects.
- **Challenges:** They may struggle with delegating tasks or being overly critical when standards are not met.

Scorpio and Personal Growth

To unlock their full potential, Scorpios can benefit from embracing vulnerability and letting go of the need to control outcomes.

Tips for Personal Growth:

1. **Embrace Forgiveness:** Learn to let go of grudges and focus on moving forward.
2. **Open Up:** Share your thoughts and feelings with trusted loved ones to build deeper connections.

3. **Balance Intensity:** Channel your passionate nature into productive and creative outlets.
4. **Practice Flexibility:** Be open to alternative viewpoints and adapt to change with grace.
5. **Focus on Self-Care:** Prioritize emotional well-being and learn to step back from situations that drain your energy.

Scorpio Compatibility

- **Best Matches:** Cancer, Pisces, Capricorn, and Virgo—these signs appreciate Scorpio's emotional depth, loyalty, and determination.
- **Challenging Matches:** Aquarius and Leo, whose free-spirited or assertive natures may clash with Scorpio's intensity and need for control.

Conclusion

Scorpios are passionate, loyal, and resourceful individuals who bring depth and intensity to every aspect of their lives. While their powerful emotions and guarded nature can sometimes pose challenges, their determination, resilience, and transformative energy make them extraordinary friends, partners, and leaders. By embracing vulnerability and focusing on growth, Scorpios can unlock their full potential and create a life filled with meaning and success.

Introduce

2025 is set to be a dynamic and transformative year for Scorpio (October 23 – November 21). Ruled by Pluto and Mars, Scorpios thrive on change, resilience, and emotional depth, and this year will call upon these strengths as you navigate exciting opportunities and challenges. With planetary influences highlighting themes of personal growth, relationship depth, and career success, 2025 encourages you to harness your passion and intuition to create meaningful progress.

This year's celestial movements emphasize balance, requiring you to integrate your need for control with a willingness to embrace vulnerability and collaboration. As you grow through these lessons, you'll experience transformative success and deeper connections in all areas of life.

Overall Energy for Scorpio in 2025

The year begins with Jupiter in Taurus, your opposite sign, emphasizing partnerships, collaboration, and mutual growth. This energy will encourage you to focus on building meaningful relationships, whether personal or professional and finding a balance between independence and cooperation. Saturn in Pisces continues to highlight creativity and self-expression, encouraging you to channel your emotions into artistic or personal endeavors that align with your true self.

Pluto's transit into Aquarius introduces themes of home, family, and emotional grounding, urging you to transform your inner world and strengthen your roots. As Jupiter transitions into Gemini mid-year, your focus will shift toward intellectual pursuits, communication, and expanding your network. The combination of these influences provides Scorpio with opportunities for profound growth, emotional healing, and success.

Career and Ambition

2025 is a year of focus, determination, and success in your professional life. Jupiter in Taurus emphasizes collaboration and teamwork, making it a favorable time to work closely with others to achieve shared goals. Mid-year, as Jupiter moves into Gemini, you'll find opportunities to innovate and broaden your skill set, allowing you to thrive in fast-paced or intellectually stimulating environments.

- **Key Opportunities:** Leadership roles, networking, and long-term career projects are well-supported this year. Scorpios will excel in fields requiring problem-solving, creativity, and emotional intelligence.

- **Challenges:** Your natural intensity and perfectionism may create tension in collaborative settings. Be mindful of balancing assertiveness with diplomacy.

Tips for Career Success in 2025:

1. Build strong professional relationships by being open to new perspectives and feedback.
2. Take calculated risks, especially in the latter half of the year, to explore innovative career paths or strategies.
3. Use Pluto's transformative energy to align your work with your passions and values.

Finance and Wealth

Your financial outlook in 2025 is stable and promising, with opportunities for growth and long-term planning. Jupiter in Taurus during the first half of the year emphasizes steady financial progress, making it a great time to focus on saving, investing, and managing resources wisely. The transition to Gemini mid-year encourages exploring new income streams or diversifying your financial strategies.

- **Key Opportunities:** Financial gains may come from partnerships, investments, or creative ventures that align with your skills and values.

- **Challenges:** Be cautious of impulsive financial decisions, particularly when pursuing new opportunities in the latter half of the year.

Tips for Financial Success in 2025:

1. Prioritize saving and stick to a disciplined budget.
2. Seek advice before making major financial commitments or investments.
3. Focus on long-term financial stability over short-term gratification.

Love and Relationships

Relationships take center stage for Scorpio in 2025, with Jupiter in Taurus emphasizing partnerships and intimacy. This year encourages you to deepen existing connections, heal past wounds, and embrace vulnerability in your interactions. The transformative energy of Pluto in Aquarius inspires a renewed focus on family and emotional security, urging you to build relationships that align with your authentic self.

- **For Singles:** The first half of the year may bring opportunities to meet someone through work, social events, or shared interests. Mid-year, the Gemini energy supports lighthearted conversations and intellectual connections, making it a favorable time for new beginnings.

- **For Those in Relationships:** Focus on strengthening trust and resolving any lingering issues with your partner. Open communication and shared experiences will help you grow closer.

Challenges in Love:

- Emotional intensity or jealousy may create tension if not balanced with trust and understanding.
- Your desire for control may clash with the need for compromise in partnerships.

Tips for Love and Relationships in 2025:

1. Practice active listening and empathy to strengthen emotional bonds.
2. Be open to vulnerability and trust in your partner's intentions.
3. Use the transformative energy of Pluto to heal past wounds and embrace a brighter future.

Health and Wellness

Health is a key focus for Scorpio in 2025, with Saturn in Pisces urging you to establish sustainable wellness routines that nurture both body and mind.

- **Physical Health:** The steady energy of Jupiter in Taurus supports grounding practices like yoga, meditation, or mindful eating. Regular exercise and a balanced diet will enhance your physical vitality.

- **Mental and Emotional Health:** Pluto in Aquarius encourages self-reflection and emotional healing. Use this energy to release old patterns or beliefs that no longer serve you.

Challenges in Health:

Balancing work, relationships, and self-care may feel challenging at times. Prioritize rest and avoid overextending yourself.

Tips for Health and Wellness in 2025:

1. Incorporate mindfulness practices into your daily routine to reduce stress and improve focus.
2. Stay consistent with fitness and nutrition, but avoid pushing yourself too hard.
3. Dedicate time to hobbies or creative outlets that bring you joy and relaxation.

Personal Growth and Spirituality

2025 is a transformative year for Scorpio, offering opportunities for profound personal and spiritual growth. Pluto's influence encourages introspection, emotional healing, and aligning with your true purpose.

- **Key Themes:** Letting go of the past, embracing change, and stepping into your power will define your journey this year.
- **Opportunities for Growth:** Explore creative or spiritual pursuits that resonate with your soul. Use your intuition and emotional depth to guide your decisions.

Tips for Personal Growth in 2025:

1. Trust your instincts and embrace change as an opportunity for growth.
2. Focus on progress, not perfection, as you work toward your goals.
3. Practice gratitude and celebrate your achievements, no matter how small.

Key Dates for Scorpio in 2025

- **March 15:** A New Moon in Pisces highlights creativity and emotional healing, making it an ideal time for new beginnings.
- **May 22:** A Full Moon in Sagittarius brings clarity to your goals and inspires action.
- **October 13:** A New Moon in Libra encourages balance and harmony in relationships.

Challenges for Scorpio in 2025

- Balancing your intense emotional nature with the need for collaboration and compromise.
- Letting go of control and trusting others to contribute meaningfully to shared goals.
- Managing stress from juggling personal and professional responsibilities.

Conclusion

2025 is a year of transformation, growth, and empowerment for Scorpio. By embracing change, deepening your relationships, and focusing on personal growth, you'll navigate this year with resilience and confidence. Use your intuition, passion, and determination to overcome challenges and create a life that aligns with your values and dreams.

Scorpio, this year is your opportunity to shine—step forward with strength and purpose!

January

January 2025 is a month of focus, reflection, and progress for Scorpio. With the Sun in Capricorn for most of the month, the energy emphasizes discipline, long-term planning, and laying a strong foundation for success. This is an ideal time to align your goals with your values and take strategic steps toward personal and professional growth.

Work

January highlights productivity and strategic planning in Scorpio's professional life.

- **Opportunities:** The Capricorn energy supports focus and discipline, making this a great time to tackle complex tasks, refine ongoing projects, and set long-term career goals. Mid-month offers opportunities for collaboration or leadership roles.
- **Challenges:** Avoid letting perfectionism or overanalyzing slow your progress. Trust your instincts and take calculated risks.

Advice: Use the structured Capricorn energy to prioritize your goals and stay consistent in your efforts.

Finance

Your financial outlook in January emphasizes careful planning and long-term security.

- **Opportunities:** This is a favorable time to revisit your budget, focus on savings, and explore stable investment opportunities. Rewards may come from disciplined financial decisions made in the past.
- **Challenges:** Avoid impulsive purchases, particularly on luxury items or social activities.

Advice: Stick to a realistic budget and focus on building a secure financial future.

Love

January brings depth and reflection to Scorpio's love life.

- **For Singles:** This is a time for introspection, helping you clarify what you truly want in a partner. Romantic opportunities may arise through work or shared interests, but take your time to build trust and connection.
- **For Those in Relationships:** Focus on strengthening emotional intimacy with your

partner. Honest communication and thoughtful gestures will deepen your bond.

Advice: Be authentic and patient in your interactions. Use this month to nurture emotional stability and connection.

Health

Health-wise, January encourages Scorpio to focus on balance and consistency.

- **Strengths:** The Capricorn energy supports creating or refining routines that promote both physical and mental well-being. Activities like yoga, meditation, or regular exercise will help you stay grounded.
- **Challenges:** Stress from work or personal responsibilities may affect your energy levels if not managed carefully.

Advice: Incorporate mindfulness practices into your daily routine. Ensure you're eating well, staying hydrated, and getting enough rest.

Be Careful

- **Overworking:** Avoid overloading yourself with responsibilities, as this could lead to burnout.

- **Emotional Intensity:** Manage your emotions to avoid unnecessary conflicts or misunderstandings.
- **Neglecting Self-Care:** Balance your focus on work with relaxation and self-care to maintain well-being.

Advice

1. **Plan Strategically:** Use Capricorn's disciplined energy to set clear and actionable goals for the year ahead.
2. **Strengthen Relationships:** Focus on building trust and connection in your personal and professional relationships.
3. **Practice Balance:** Maintain harmony between ambition and self-care to sustain your energy and clarity.

Additional Tips

- **Lucky Days:** January 8, 17, and 29 – Ideal for decision-making, creative pursuits, or strengthening relationships.
- **Lucky Color:** Burgundy – This color symbolizes passion, strength, and grounding.
- **Affirmation for January:** *"I align my actions with my purpose, creating harmony and success in all areas of my life."*

January 2025 is a month of grounding and preparation for Scorpio. By focusing on thoughtful planning, meaningful connections, and self-care, you'll set the stage for a transformative and fulfilling year ahead.

February

February 2025 is a month of creativity, connection, and emotional growth for Scorpio. With the Sun in Aquarius for most of the month, the focus shifts to your relationships, innovation, and exploring new ways of thinking. As the Sun transitions into Pisces later in February, the energy becomes more introspective and creative, encouraging you to nurture your emotional well-being and align with your inner passions.

Work

February emphasizes collaboration and innovation in Scorpio's professional life.

- **Opportunities:** The Aquarius energy supports teamwork, brainstorming, and embracing new technologies or strategies to enhance your productivity. Late in the month, the Pisces energy inspires creativity, making it a great time to tackle artistic or emotionally meaningful projects.
- **Challenges:** Balancing your intensity with Aquarius' lighthearted energy may feel challenging. Avoid becoming too rigid in your approach.

Advice: Be open to new perspectives and innovative ideas. Use Pisces' imaginative energy later in the month to bring fresh solutions to your work.

Finance

Your financial outlook in February highlights discipline and gradual growth.

- **Opportunities:** Financial gains may come from collaborative ventures or creative projects. This is also a good time to reassess your savings goals and make adjustments for future stability.
- **Challenges:** Avoid impulsive spending, particularly during moments of excitement or stress.

Advice: Stick to a clear financial plan and focus on long-term stability rather than short-term indulgences.

Love

February brings warmth and depth to Scorpio's love life, with Venus enhancing emotional connection and harmony.

- **For Singles:** Social gatherings, work connections, or shared interests may lead to promising romantic encounters. Look for partners who resonate with your values and intellectual curiosity.

- **For Those in Relationships:** Focus on strengthening communication and emotional intimacy with your partner. Late February is ideal for planning special moments or discussing plans.

Advice: Be authentic and vulnerable in your interactions. Use the Pisces energy to deepen emotional bonds and celebrate love in its many forms.

Health

Health-wise, February encourages Scorpio to focus on balance and maintaining emotional well-being.

- **Strengths:** The Aquarius energy supports staying active and engaging in group activities that boost both mental and physical health.
- **Challenges:** Stress from juggling responsibilities may affect your energy levels if not managed effectively.

Advice: Incorporate relaxation techniques like yoga, meditation, or creative hobbies to reduce stress. Maintain consistency in your exercise and nutrition routines to sustain vitality.

<u>*Be Careful*</u>

- **Overthinking:** Avoid dwelling on past mistakes or uncertainties, as this could drain your emotional energy.
- **Impulsiveness:** Think carefully before making major financial or personal decisions.
- **Neglecting Balance:** Balance your ambitious goals with self-care to avoid burnout.

<u>*Advice*</u>

1. **Embrace Collaboration:** Use Aquarius' dynamic energy to build meaningful connections and explore innovative ideas.
2. **Nurture Creativity:** Tap into Pisces' imaginative influence to channel your emotions into productive and fulfilling outlets.
3. **Focus on Self-Care:** Balance productivity with relaxation to maintain your physical and emotional well-being.

<u>*Additional Tips*</u>

- **Lucky Days:** February 9, 16, and 27 – Ideal for networking, decision-making, or creative pursuits.
- **Lucky Color:** Aquamarine – This color symbolizes clarity, calmness, and emotional healing.

- **Affirmation for February:** *"I balance my ambition with self-care, creating harmony and success in all areas of my life."*

February 2025 is a month of connection and creativity for Scorpio. By focusing on collaboration, thoughtful planning, and self-care, you'll navigate this vibrant period with confidence and clarity.

March

March 2025 is a month of reflection, emotional growth, and meaningful progress for Scorpio. With the Sun in Pisces for most of the month, the energy encourages introspection, creativity, and nurturing of your emotional well-being. As the Sun transitions into Aries later in March, the focus shifts to action, ambition, and taking decisive steps toward your goals. This combination of imaginative reflection and bold action makes March a dynamic and transformative time.

Work

March emphasizes creativity and strategic planning in Scorpio's professional life.

- **Opportunities:** The Pisces energy supports innovative thinking, making it a favorable time for tackling creative or emotionally meaningful projects. The Aries's influence later in the month motivates them to take bold steps, present ideas, or seek leadership roles.
- **Challenges:** Balancing your introspective tendencies with the need for decisive action may feel challenging. Avoid overanalyzing and trust your instincts.

Advice: Use Pisces energy to refine your strategies and Aries energy to execute them with confidence. Focus on clear communication and collaboration to achieve success.

Finance

Your financial outlook in March emphasizes thoughtful planning and potential gains.

- **Opportunities:** Financial rewards may come from creative ventures, partnerships, or efforts you've been nurturing in recent months. This is also a good time to reevaluate your financial goals and align your budget with your priorities.
- **Challenges:** Avoid impulsive spending, particularly during Aries season when high energy might tempt indulgence.

Advice: Stick to a disciplined financial plan and focus on long-term stability. Seek professional advice if considering significant financial decisions.

Love

March brings emotional depth and harmony to Scorpio's love life, with Venus fostering connection and intimacy.

- **For Singles:** Romantic opportunities may arise through shared interests, creative activities, or social events. Emotional compatibility will play a key role in forming meaningful connections.
- **For Those in Relationships:** Focus on deepening emotional intimacy and resolving any lingering misunderstandings with your partner. Late March is ideal for reigniting passion and creating exciting new memories together.

Advice: Be authentic and open in your interactions. Use Pisces energy to nurture emotional bonds and Aries energy to celebrate your connection.

Health

Health-wise, March encourages Scorpio to focus on balance and emotional well-being.

- **Strengths:** The Pisces energy inspires self-care practices like meditation, journaling, or spending time in nature. The Aries's influence later in the month supports physical activity and boosts energy levels.
- **Challenges:** Stress from juggling responsibilities may affect your energy if not managed effectively.

Advice: Incorporate mindfulness techniques into your daily routine to stay grounded. Focus on maintaining a balanced diet, staying hydrated, and ensuring you get enough rest.

Be Careful

- **Overthinking:** Avoid dwelling on uncertainties or trying to control every outcome. Trust the process.
- **Neglecting Balance:** Balance your reflective tendencies with moments of action and social engagement.
- **Impulsiveness:** Think carefully before making major financial or personal decisions, especially during Aries season.

Advice

1. **Reflect and Create:** Use Pisces energy to connect with your inner self and channel emotions into creative and productive outlets.
2. **Take Bold Steps:** Embrace Aries energy to act decisively on well-thought-out plans and pursue new opportunities.
3. **Nurture Relationships:** Invest time in meaningful connections and express appreciation for your loved ones.

Additional Tips

- **Lucky Days:** March 10, 19, and 29 – Ideal for decision-making, creative projects, or deepening relationships.
- **Lucky Color:** Deep Blue – This color symbolizes intuition, clarity, and focus.
- **Affirmation for March:** _"I balance introspection with action, creating harmony and success in my life."_

March 2025 is a month of emotional growth and dynamic action for Scorpio. By focusing on meaningful connections, thoughtful planning, and self-care, you'll navigate this transformative period with confidence and clarity.

April

April 2025 is a month of action, transformation, and building momentum for Scorpio. With the Sun in Aries for most of the month, the focus is on assertiveness, leadership, and taking charge of your goals. As the Sun transitions into Taurus later in April, the energy shifts toward stability, grounding, and nurturing important relationships. This combination of fiery ambition and practical grounding makes April a powerful time to make meaningful progress in your life.

Work

April emphasizes leadership and productivity in Scorpio's professional life.

- **Opportunities:** The Aries energy supports bold initiatives, tackling challenging projects, and stepping into leadership roles. Mid-month offers opportunities to pitch new ideas or take decisive action on career goals. The Taurus influence later in the month encourages steady progress and lays a solid foundation for future success.
- **Challenges:** Balancing your intensity with Aries' fast-paced energy may feel challenging. Avoid rushing decisions without considering all factors.

Advice: Use Aries' dynamic energy to make bold moves and Taurus' steady energy to ensure your actions are sustainable and impactful.

Finance

Your financial outlook in April highlights growth and careful management.

- **Opportunities:** Financial gains may come from investments, collaborations, or rewards for past efforts. This is a favorable time to reassess your budget and plan for future financial goals.
- **Challenges:** Avoid impulsive spending, especially during moments of excitement or stress.

Advice: Focus on saving and prioritize financial stability. Use Taurus' practical energy to make thoughtful decisions and align your finances with your long-term plans.

Love

April brings warmth and passion to Scorpio's love life, with Venus enhancing connection and intimacy.

- **For Singles:** Social events, work, or shared activities may lead to promising romantic connections. Confidence and authenticity will play a key role in attracting meaningful relationships.

- **For Those in Relationships:** Focus on nurturing trust and emotional closeness with your partner. Plan special moments to celebrate your bond and discuss shared goals for the future.

Advice: Be open and genuine in your interactions. Use Taurus' grounding energy later in the month to strengthen emotional stability in your relationships.

Health

Health-wise, April encourages Scorpio to maintain consistency and prioritize self-care amidst a busy schedule.

- **Strengths:** The Aries energy inspires physical activity and motivation, making it a great time to enhance your fitness routine or try new exercises.
- **Challenges:** Overexertion or neglecting rest during the fast-paced Aries season may lead to fatigue if not managed properly.

Advice: Incorporate relaxation techniques into your daily routine to stay balanced. Focus on maintaining a healthy diet, staying hydrated, and ensuring you get enough sleep to recharge.

Be Careful

- **Impulsiveness:** Avoid making hasty decisions in work or financial matters without thoroughly evaluating the consequences.
- **Overcommitment:** Don't take on too many responsibilities at once, as this could lead to stress or burnout.
- **Neglecting Relationships:** Balance your professional ambitions with attention to personal connections.

Advice

1. **Lead with Confidence:** Use Aries' bold energy to take charge of your goals and embrace leadership opportunities.
2. **Ground Your Actions:** As Taurus season begins, focus on building stability and ensuring your efforts are sustainable.
3. **Nurture Connections:** Strengthen emotional bonds with loved ones through thoughtful communication and meaningful gestures.

Additional Tips

- **Lucky Days:** April 9, 18, and 27 – Ideal for decision-making, creative pursuits, or fostering relationships.

- **Lucky Color:** Scarlet Red – This color symbolizes passion, confidence, and vitality.
- **Affirmation for April:** *"I take bold steps toward my goals, creating harmony and success in all areas of my life."*

April 2025 is a month of empowerment and transformation for Scorpio. By balancing ambition with thoughtful planning and nurturing meaningful connections, you'll make the most of this dynamic and fulfilling period.

May

May 2025 is a month of stability, introspection, and steady progress for Scorpio. With the Sun in Taurus for most of the month, the focus is on grounding, financial planning, and strengthening your personal and professional foundations. As the Sun transitions into Gemini later in May, the energy shifts to communication, curiosity, and expanding your horizons. This blend of stability and adaptability makes May an excellent time for creating long-term strategies while embracing dynamic opportunities.

Work

May emphasizes focus and collaboration in Scorpio's professional life.

- **Opportunities:** Taurus Energy supports refining ongoing projects, building strong relationships with colleagues, and establishing a secure footing in your career. Late in the month, the Gemini energy inspires brainstorming, networking, and exploring innovative approaches to your work.
- **Challenges:** Avoid stubbornness or becoming too fixed in your routines, especially as Gemini's dynamic energy encourages flexibility.

Advice: Use Taurus' steady energy to complete important tasks and Gemini's influence to explore new ideas and collaborations.

Finance

Your financial outlook in May emphasizes cautious growth and strategic planning.

- **Opportunities:** Financial gains may come from investments, bonuses, or creative ventures. This is also a good time to reassess your budget and set realistic financial goals for the months ahead.
- **Challenges:** Avoid overspending, especially on luxuries or impulsive purchases during moments of social excitement.

Advice: Focus on saving and building long-term financial stability. Consider seeking advice before making major financial decisions.

Love

May brings emotional stability and growth to Scorpio's love life.

- **For Singles:** This is a favorable time for meeting someone through work, shared interests, or community activities. Emotional compatibility will be a key factor in forming new connections.

- **For Those in Relationships:** Focus on building trust and stability in your partnership. Late May is ideal for planning adventures or engaging in meaningful conversations to deepen your bond.

Advice: Be patient and authentic in your interactions. Use Taurus energy to nurture emotional stability and Gemini energy to keep your relationships lighthearted and exciting.

Health

Health-wise, May encourages Scorpio to maintain consistency and balance in their wellness routines.

- **Strengths:** The Taurus energy supports grounding practices like yoga, meditation, or outdoor activities that promote relaxation and resilience.
- **Challenges:** Stress from juggling responsibilities may affect your energy levels if not managed effectively.

Advice: Incorporate relaxation techniques into your daily routine. Focus on maintaining a healthy diet, staying hydrated, and ensuring adequate rest to recharge your body and mind.

<u>*Be Careful*</u>

- **Overindulgence:** Avoid overcommitting to social activities or indulging in unhealthy habits.
- **Rigid Thinking:** Be open to new ideas and flexible approaches, especially as Gemini energy encourages adaptability.
- **Neglecting Balance:** Ensure you're prioritizing self-care amidst your busy schedule.

<u>*Advice*</u>

1. **Ground Yourself:** Use Taurus energy to focus on creating stability in your career, relationships, and finances.
2. **Stay Curious:** Embrace Gemini's dynamic influence to explore new ideas, connections, and opportunities for growth.
3. **Nurture Connections:** Invest time in meaningful relationships and express appreciation for those who support you.

<u>*Additional Tips*</u>

- **Lucky Days:** May 10, 19, and 28 – Ideal for decision-making, creative pursuits, or strengthening relationships.
- **Lucky Color:** Emerald Green – This color symbolizes growth, balance, and renewal.

- **Affirmation for May:** *"I create stability and embrace new opportunities, aligning my actions with my goals and dreams."*

May 2025 is a month of balance and growth for Scorpio. By focusing on thoughtful planning, meaningful relationships, and self-care, you'll navigate this productive period with confidence and clarity.

June

June 2025 is a month of exploration, transformation, and connection for Scorpio. With the Sun in Gemini for most of the month, the focus is on communication, curiosity, and expanding your horizons. As the Sun transitions into Cancer later in June, the energy shifts to emotional depth, introspection, and nurturing relationships. This combination of intellectual stimulation and emotional connection makes June a time of dynamic growth and meaningful progress.

Work

June emphasizes adaptability and collaboration in Scorpio's professional life.

- **Opportunities:** The Gemini energy supports networking, brainstorming, and working on innovative projects. Late in the month, Cancer's influence encourages focusing on long-term strategies and nurturing supportive relationships with colleagues.
- **Challenges:** Balancing your intense focus with Gemini's fast-paced energy may feel challenging. Avoid becoming too fixated on details and embrace flexibility.

Advice: Use Gemini energy to explore new ideas and connections, and Cancer energy to align your goals with your values and build stability.

Finance

Your financial outlook in June highlights cautious planning and steady growth.

- **Opportunities:** Financial gains may come from collaborative ventures, side projects, or investments. This is also a good time to focus on saving and reassessing your financial priorities.
- **Challenges:** Avoid impulsive spending, especially during moments of social excitement or emotional decision-making.

Advice: Stick to a disciplined budget and focus on financial stability. Seek advice if considering significant investments or changes.

Love

June brings excitement and emotional depth to Scorpio's love life.

- **For Singles:** This is a favorable time for meeting someone new through social events, intellectual pursuits, or shared interests. Emotional compatibility will be key to building meaningful connections.

- **For Those in Relationships:** Focus on open communication and creating memorable experiences with your partner. The Cancer energy later in the month encourages deeper emotional intimacy.

Advice: Be authentic and attentive in your interactions. Use Gemini energy to keep things lively and Cancer energy to nurture emotional closeness.

Health

Health-wise, June encourages Scorpio to focus on emotional and physical well-being.

- **Strengths:** The Gemini energy supports staying active and engaging in activities that stimulate both the mind and body.
- **Challenges:** Stress from juggling responsibilities or overcommitting to social activities may affect your energy levels.

Advice: Incorporate relaxation techniques like meditation or journaling into your daily routine. Maintain consistency in exercise and nutrition, and prioritize rest to recharge.

- **Overcommitting:** Avoid taking on too many responsibilities, as this could lead to stress or burnout.
- **Impulsiveness:** Think carefully before making major decisions in financial or personal matters.
- **Neglecting Self-Care:** Balance your active schedule with downtime to maintain overall well-being.

Advice

1. **Explore and Adapt:** Use Gemini's dynamic energy to embrace new ideas, connections, and opportunities for growth.
2. **Focus on Depth:** Embrace Cancer's nurturing influence to strengthen relationships and align with your emotional needs.
3. **Maintain Balance:** Prioritize self-care and relaxation to sustain energy and clarity throughout the month.

Additional Tips

- **Lucky Days:** June 8, 16, and 28 – Perfect for networking, creative pursuits, or decision-making.
- **Lucky Color:** Sapphire Blue – This color symbolizes clarity, intuition, and emotional balance.

- **Affirmation for June:** *"I balance curiosity and connection, creating harmony and growth in all areas of my life."*

June 2025 is a month of exploration and emotional growth for Scorpio. By focusing on meaningful connections, thoughtful planning, and self-care, you'll navigate this transformative period with confidence and clarity.

July

July 2025 is a month of emotional depth, connection, and personal empowerment for Scorpio. With the Sun in Cancer for most of the month, the focus is on nurturing relationships, aligning with your emotional needs, and creating a sense of security in your life. As the Sun transitions into Leo later in July, the energy becomes more dynamic, encouraging you to step into the spotlight, express yourself creatively, and pursue your ambitions with confidence.

Work

July emphasizes strategic planning and creativity in Scorpio's professional life.

- **Opportunities:** The Cancer energy supports building strong professional relationships and reassessing long-term goals. Late in the month, the Leo influence inspires bold ideas and leadership opportunities, making it an excellent time to take center stage in your career.
- **Challenges:** Balancing your introspective tendencies with Leo's vibrant energy may feel challenging. Avoid overthinking decisions and trust your instincts.

Advice: Use Cancer energy to align your plans with your values and Leo energy to act decisively and embrace leadership opportunities.

Finance

Your financial outlook in July highlights cautious planning and gradual progress.

- **Opportunities:** Financial gains may come from creative projects, partnerships, or past investments. This is also a favorable time to focus on saving and setting financial goals for the future.
- **Challenges:** Avoid impulsive spending, particularly during moments of celebration or stress.

Advice: Stick to your financial plan and focus on building long-term stability. Use Leo's confidence to explore new income opportunities thoughtfully.

Love

July brings warmth and emotional connection to Scorpio's love life, with Venus enhancing intimacy and harmony.

- **For Singles:** This is a great time to meet someone new through social gatherings, creative activities, or shared emotional interests. Look for connections that resonate on a deeper level.

- **For Those in Relationships:** Focus on nurturing trust and emotional intimacy with your partner. Late July is ideal for planning special moments together to reignite passion and strengthen your bond.

Advice: Be open and genuine in your interactions. Use Cancer energy to deepen emotional bonds and Leo energy to celebrate love and connection.

Health

Health-wise, July encourages Scorpio to prioritize emotional and physical well-being.

- **Strengths:** The Cancer energy supports self-care practices like journaling, meditation, or spending time in nature. Late in the month, Leo's dynamic influence inspires physical activity and vitality.
- **Challenges:** Stress from balancing responsibilities may affect your energy levels if not managed effectively.

Advice: Incorporate relaxation techniques into your routine and focus on maintaining consistency in your wellness habits. Ensure you're staying hydrated, eating well, and getting adequate rest.

<u>*Be Careful*</u>

- **Overexertion:** Avoid taking on too many responsibilities at once, as this could lead to stress or burnout.
- **Emotional Intensity:** Manage your emotions to avoid conflicts or misunderstandings in relationships.
- **Impulsiveness:** Think carefully before making major financial or personal decisions.

<u>*Advice*</u>

1. **Embrace Emotional Depth:** Use Cancer energy to reflect on your needs and nurture meaningful relationships.
2. **Step into the Spotlight:** As Leo season begins, focus on expressing yourself creatively and confidently pursuing your ambitions.
3. **Balance and Self-Care:** Prioritize your physical and emotional well-being to maintain energy and clarity throughout the month.

<u>*Additional Tips*</u>

- **Lucky Days:** July 9, 17, and 29 – Ideal for decision-making, creative projects, or strengthening relationships.

- **Lucky Color:** Ruby Red – This color symbolizes passion, strength, and vitality.
- **Affirmation for July:** *"I align my emotions with my actions, creating harmony and success in all areas of my life."*

July 2025 is a month of connection and empowerment for Scorpio. By focusing on emotional growth, meaningful relationships, and personal goals, you'll navigate this transformative period with confidence and clarity.

August

August 2025 is a month of empowerment, self-expression, and transformation for Scorpio. With the Sun in Leo for most of the month, the focus is on leadership, creativity, and embracing your ambitions. As the Sun transitions into Virgo later in August, the energy shifts toward organization, refinement, and building a strong foundation for future success. This combination of boldness and practicality makes August an exciting time for personal growth and professional progress.

Work

August emphasizes leadership and strategic action in Scorpio's professional life.

- **Opportunities:** The Leo energy supports showcasing your talents, taking on leadership roles, and pursuing bold ideas. Late in the month, Virgo's influence encourages attention to detail and refining your strategies to achieve long-term goals.
- **Challenges:** Balancing Leo's dynamic energy with Virgo's meticulousness may feel challenging. Avoid becoming overly critical of yourself or others.

Advice: Use Leo's bold energy to embrace opportunities and Virgo's grounded approach to ensure your plans are actionable and sustainable.

Finance

Your financial outlook in August highlights growth and careful planning.

- **Opportunities:** Financial gains may come from creative projects, promotions, or investments. This is also a good time to reevaluate your budget and align your spending with your goals.
- **Challenges:** Avoid impulsive spending during moments of excitement or overconfidence.

Advice: Stick to a disciplined financial plan and focus on saving for future investments or goals. Use Virgo's practical energy to make thoughtful financial decisions.

Love

August brings passion and excitement to Scorpio's love life, with Venus enhancing connection and harmony.

- **For Singles:** This is a favorable time to meet someone new through creative activities, social events, or work-related gatherings. Your confidence and charisma will attract meaningful connections.

- **For Those in Relationships:** Focus on reigniting passion and celebrating your bond with your partner. Late August is ideal for discussing shared goals and nurturing emotional stability.

Advice: Be authentic and expressive in your interactions. Use Leo energy to celebrate love and Virgo energy to deepen trust and emotional intimacy.

Health

Health-wise, August encourages Scorpio to maintain energy and focus on self-care.

- **Strengths:** The Leo energy inspires physical activity and vitality, making it a great time to enhance your fitness routine or try new exercises.
- **Challenges:** Overexertion or neglecting rest during a busy schedule may lead to fatigue if not managed carefully.

Advice: Incorporate relaxation techniques like yoga or meditation into your routine. Ensure you're staying hydrated, eating balanced meals, and prioritizing adequate rest to recharge.

Be Careful

- **Overconfidence:** Avoid taking on more than you can handle, as this could lead to stress or burnout.
- **Impulsiveness:** Think carefully before making significant financial or personal decisions.
- **Neglecting Details:** Balance your big-picture vision with attention to the finer points, especially as Virgo season begins.

Advice

1. **Step into Leadership:** Use Leo's bold energy to embrace opportunities, showcase your talents, and pursue your ambitions with confidence.
2. **Refine Your Goals:** As Virgo season begins, focus on organizing your plans and aligning your actions with your long-term vision.
3. **Prioritize Balance:** Maintain harmony between your ambitions and self-care to stay energized and grounded.

Additional Tips

- **Lucky Days:** August 11, 19, and 28 – Perfect for decision-making, creative projects, or fostering relationships.
- **Lucky Color:** Gold – This color symbolizes success, confidence, and vitality.

- **Affirmation for August:** *"I embrace my strengths and align my actions with my purpose, creating harmony and growth in my life."*

August 2025 is a month of bold action and thoughtful planning for Scorpio. By focusing on self-expression, meaningful connections, and disciplined progress, you'll make the most of this dynamic and fulfilling period.

September

September 2025 is a month of introspection, focus, and preparation for Scorpio. With the Sun in Virgo for most of the month, the energy emphasizes organization, refinement, and aligning your plans with your long-term goals. As the Sun transitions into Libra later in September, the focus shifts to balance, relationships, and collaborative efforts. This combination of practicality and diplomacy creates opportunities for growth in both personal and professional aspects of your life.

Work

September emphasizes productivity and precision in Scorpio's professional life.

- **Opportunities:** Virgo Energy supports refining ongoing projects, improving work processes, and addressing details that need attention. Late in the month, the Libra influence encourages teamwork, networking, and building harmonious professional relationships.
- **Challenges:** Avoid becoming overly critical of yourself or others as you work through tasks. Balance your intense focus with flexibility.

Advice: Use Virgo's meticulous energy to complete important tasks and Libra's diplomatic influence to strengthen collaborations and professional relationships.

Finance

Your financial outlook in September highlights discipline and careful planning.

- **Opportunities:** Financial gains may come from efforts made earlier in the year, and this is a favorable time to reassess your budget and savings goals.
- **Challenges:** Avoid impulsive spending or overanalyzing financial decisions to the point of inaction.

Advice: Stick to a clear financial plan and focus on building long-term stability. Seek professional advice if considering major investments or changes.

Love

September brings depth and harmony to Scorpio's love life, with Venus enhancing connection and emotional stability.

- **For Singles:** This is a good time to reflect on what you want in a partner and focus on building meaningful connections. Social gatherings or intellectual pursuits may lead to promising romantic opportunities.

- **For Those in Relationships:** Focus on strengthening trust and communication with your partner. Late September is ideal for resolving misunderstandings and nurturing emotional intimacy.

Advice: Be open and attentive in your interactions. Use Virgo's grounding energy to nurture emotional stability and Libra's influence to celebrate love and connection.

Health

Health-wise, September encourages Scorpio to focus on balance and maintaining consistency in wellness routines.

- **Strengths:** The Virgo energy supports mindful practices like yoga, meditation, or healthy eating habits that enhance both physical and mental well-being.
- **Challenges:** Stress from work or personal responsibilities may affect your energy levels if not managed effectively.

Advice: Incorporate relaxation techniques into your daily routine to stay grounded. Focus on maintaining a balanced diet, staying hydrated, and getting adequate rest.

Be Careful

- **Overanalyzing:** Avoid dwelling on imperfections or trying to control every detail. Focus on progress rather than perfection.
- **Neglecting Balance:** Ensure you're devoting time to both personal relationships and self-care alongside your professional goals.
- **Impulsiveness:** Think carefully before making major decisions in financial or personal matters.

Advice

1. **Focus on Refinement:** Use Virgo energy to align your plans with your values and ensure your goals are realistic and actionable.
2. **Foster Connections:** Embrace Libra's influence to strengthen relationships and build meaningful collaborations.
3. **Prioritize Self-Care:** Maintain harmony between your ambitions and personal well-being to sustain energy and clarity.

- **Lucky Days:** September 8, 16, and 27 – Ideal for decision-making, creative pursuits, or fostering relationships.
- **Lucky Color:** Forest Green – This color symbolizes growth, balance, and renewal.
- **Affirmation for September:** *"I align my actions with my values, creating harmony and success in all areas of my life."*

September 2025 is a month of preparation and focus for Scorpio. By balancing introspection with action and nurturing meaningful connections, you'll navigate this productive period with confidence and clarity.

October

October 2025 is a month of transformation, connection, and empowerment for Scorpio. With the Sun in Libra for most of the month, the focus is on relationships, balance, and collaboration. As the Sun transitions into your sign later in October, the energy becomes intense and introspective, encouraging you to embrace your power, set bold goals, and work toward personal transformation. This blend of harmony and passion makes October a pivotal month for growth and success.

Work

October emphasizes collaboration and strategic planning in Scorpio's professional life.

- **Opportunities:** The Libra energy supports teamwork, networking, and creating harmony in workplace dynamics. As the Sun enters Scorpio later in the month, you'll feel empowered to take control of your career path, address challenges, and pursue leadership roles.
- **Challenges:** Balancing Libra's diplomatic energy with Scorpio's assertiveness may feel tricky. Avoid dominating discussions or becoming overly critical of others.

Advice: Use Libra's influence to build connections and Scorpio's energy to make decisive moves that align with your long-term goals.

Finance

Your financial outlook in October highlights thoughtful planning and potential growth.

- **Opportunities:** Financial gains may come from collaborative ventures, investments, or rewards from past efforts. This is a favorable time to reassess your financial priorities and align them with your future goals.
- **Challenges:** Avoid impulsive spending, especially on luxuries or social events, as Libra season may tempt indulgence.

Advice: Focus on saving and strategic investments. Use Scorpio's transformative energy to explore new ways to grow your wealth.

Love

October brings warmth and intensity to Scorpio's love life, with Venus enhancing connection and passion.

- **For Singles:** This is a great time to attract new romantic interests, particularly through social gatherings, professional networks, or shared hobbies. Late October's Scorpio energy amplifies your magnetism, making it a favorable time for deeper connections.

- **For Those in Relationships:** Focus on nurturing trust and intimacy with your partner. Late October is ideal for deepening emotional bonds and reigniting passion.

Advice: Be authentic and open in your interactions. Use Libra energy to foster harmony and Scorpio energy to deepen emotional and physical intimacy.

Health

Health-wise, October encourages Scorpio to focus on balance and emotional well-being.

- **Strengths:** The Libra energy supports practices like yoga, mindfulness, or light exercise that promote relaxation and balance. As the month progresses, Scorpio's influence inspires transformative habits that strengthen your physical and mental health.
- **Challenges:** Stress from juggling responsibilities or emotional intensity may affect your energy levels if not managed effectively.

Advice: Prioritize self-care and incorporate relaxation techniques into your daily routine. Maintain consistency in exercise and nutrition while dedicating time for rest.

Be Careful

- **Emotional Intensity:** Avoid letting strong emotions or jealousy affect your relationships. Practice mindfulness to stay grounded.
- **Impulsiveness:** Think carefully before making significant decisions in financial or personal matters.
- **Neglecting Balance:** Ensure you're giving equal attention to your goals, relationships, and self-care.

Advice

1. **Build Connections:** Use Libra's harmonious energy to strengthen relationships and foster collaboration.
2. **Embrace Transformation:** As Scorpio season begins, focus on personal growth, setting bold goals, and embracing your inner power.
3. **Prioritize Balance:** Maintain harmony by dedicating time to self-care and meaningful relationships.

Additional Tips

- **Lucky Days:** October 9, 17, and 29 – Ideal for decision-making, creative pursuits, or strengthening relationships.

- **Lucky Color:** Crimson Red – This color symbolizes passion, strength, and transformation.
- **Affirmation for October:** *"I balance connection and transformation, creating harmony and success in all areas of my life."*

October 2025 is a month of growth and empowerment for Scorpio. By focusing on meaningful connections, thoughtful planning, and personal transformation, you'll navigate this dynamic period with confidence and clarity.

November

November 2025 is a month of introspection, transformation, and personal empowerment for Scorpio. With the Sun in your sign for most of the month, you'll feel a surge of confidence, focus, and determination. This is your time to embrace change, take charge of your goals, and align with your true purpose. As the Sun transitions into Sagittarius later in November, the energy shifts toward optimism, exploration, and broadening your horizons.

Work

November emphasizes focus, strategy, and bold decision-making in Scorpio's professional life.

- **Opportunities:** Scorpio Energy supports tackling complex projects, pursuing leadership roles, and aligning your career with your long-term vision. Late in the month, Sagittarius' influence inspires creative thinking and networking opportunities.
- **Challenges:** Balancing your intensity with Sagittarius' free-spirited energy may feel challenging. Avoid becoming too fixated on details or perfection.

Advice: Use Scorpio's transformative power to refine your plans and Sagittarius' optimism to embrace new opportunities with confidence.

Finance

Your financial outlook in November highlights cautious growth and long-term planning.

- **Opportunities:** Financial gains may come from investments, rewards for past efforts, or strategic decision-making. This is a favorable time to review your financial strategies and explore new income opportunities.
- **Challenges:** Avoid impulsive spending or taking unnecessary risks, especially as the Sagittarius season encourages spontaneity.

Advice: Stick to a disciplined financial plan and focus on building stability. Consider seeking advice if making significant financial decisions.

Love

November brings depth and passion to Scorpio's love life, with Venus enhancing connection and emotional intimacy.

- **For Singles:** This is a powerful time to attract meaningful connections, particularly through work, social events, or shared interests. Look for someone who resonates with your emotional depth and values.

- **For Those in Relationships:** Focus on deepening trust and resolving any lingering issues with your partner. Late November is ideal for planning adventures or introducing excitement into your relationship.

Advice: Be authentic and vulnerable in your interactions. Use Scorpio's intensity to nurture emotional bonds and Sagittarius' adventurous spirit to keep things fresh and exciting.

Health

Health-wise, November encourages Scorpio to focus on balance and emotional well-being.

- **Strengths:** The Scorpio energy inspires transformative habits and self-care practices that strengthen your physical and mental health. The Sagittarius influence later in the month encourages physical activity and exploring new ways to stay fit.
- **Challenges:** Emotional stress or overexertion may impact your energy levels if not managed effectively.

Advice: Prioritize relaxation. Incorporate mindfulness techniques, stay hydrated, and maintain consistency in your wellness routines to recharge.

Be Careful

- **Emotional Intensity:** Avoid letting strong emotions like jealousy or frustration impact your relationships or decisions.
- **Overthinking:** Trust your instincts and avoid getting stuck in perfectionist tendencies.
- **Neglecting Rest:** Balance your active schedule with adequate downtime to maintain energy and clarity.

Advice

1. **Embrace Transformation:** Use Scorpio energy to align with your goals, embrace change, and step into your power.
2. **Expand Your Horizons:** As Sagittarius season begins, focus on exploring new opportunities and broadening your perspective.
3. **Prioritize Self-Care:** Maintain a balanced routine that supports your physical and emotional well-being.

- **Lucky Days:** November 8, 16, and 27 – Ideal for introspection, decision-making, or creative pursuits.
- **Lucky Color:** Deep Maroon – This color symbolizes passion, resilience, and transformation.
- **Affirmation for November:** *"I embrace change and align my actions with my highest purpose, creating harmony and success in my life."*

November 2025 is a month of transformation and empowerment for Scorpio. By focusing on meaningful connections, thoughtful planning, and self-care, you'll navigate this transformative period with confidence and clarity.

December

December 2025 is a month of reflection, celebration, and forward planning for Scorpio. With the Sun in Sagittarius for most of the month, the energy encourages exploration, optimism, and connecting with others. As the Sun transitions into Capricorn later in December, the focus shifts toward grounding, practicality, and setting long-term goals. This combination of adventurous spirit and disciplined preparation makes December an ideal time to celebrate your achievements while laying the foundation for a successful 2026.

Work

December emphasizes collaboration and strategic planning in Scorpio's professional life.

- **Opportunities:** The Sagittarius energy supports networking, brainstorming, and creative problem-solving. This is a great time to explore new ideas, attend professional events, or solidify partnerships. The Capricorn influence later in the month inspires structure, making it ideal for planning career goals and aligning your actions with your ambitions.

- **Challenges:** Balancing your desire for exploration with the need for focus may feel challenging. Avoid spreading yourself too thin.

Advice: Use Sagittarius energy to explore dynamic opportunities and Capricorn energy to create actionable plans for long-term success.

Finance

Your financial outlook in December highlights balance and thoughtful decision-making.

- **Opportunities:** Financial gains may come from year-end bonuses, rewards for past efforts, or investments. This is a favorable time to reassess your budget and prepare for major expenses or savings goals in the new year.
- **Challenges:** Avoid overspending on gifts, travel, or social activities during the holiday season.

Advice: Stick to a disciplined budget and focus on building financial stability. Plan for future goals while enjoying the festive season responsibly.

Love

December brings warmth and connection to Scorpio's love life, with Venus enhancing intimacy and harmony.

- **For Singles:** Social gatherings, travel, or networking events may lead to exciting romantic opportunities. Focus on building connections with people who share your passions and values.
- **For Those in Relationships:** Celebrate your bond by planning thoughtful gestures, shared experiences, or discussions about your future together. Late December is ideal for deepening emotional intimacy and creating lasting memories.

Advice: Be open and attentive in your interactions. Use Sagittarius energy to keep things lively and Capricorn energy to nurture stability in your relationships.

Health

Health-wise, December encourages Scorpio to balance activity and rest for overall well-being.

- **Strengths:** The Sagittarius energy supports physical activity and maintaining a positive mindset, making it a great time for outdoor activities or fitness routines. Capricorn's grounding influence inspires consistency and self-discipline.
- **Challenges:** Overindulgence in holiday treats or neglecting self-care may affect your health if not moderated.

Advice: Practice moderation and prioritize relaxation. Stay consistent with healthy eating, hydration, and getting enough sleep to recharge.

Be Careful

- **Overspending:** Avoid exceeding your budget on holiday-related expenses or impulsive purchases.
- **Neglecting Rest:** Balance social commitments with downtime to maintain your energy and focus.
- **Overcommitment:** Avoid taking on too many responsibilities or projects as the year comes to a close.

Advice

1. **Celebrate and Reflect:** Use Sagittarius energy to connect with loved ones, celebrate your achievements, and reflect on your journey.
2. **Plan Strategically:** Embrace Capricorn energy to set clear, actionable goals for 2026 and prepare for future success.
3. **Prioritize Balance:** Maintain harmony by dedicating time to self-care, relationships, and thoughtful planning.

<u>*Additional Tips*</u>

- **Lucky Days:** December 7, 15, and 28 – Perfect for reflection, celebration, or decision-making.
- **Lucky Color:** Charcoal Gray – This color symbolizes strength, clarity, and grounding.
- **Affirmation for December:** *"I celebrate my journey and align my plans with my purpose, creating harmony and success in my life."*

December 2025 is a month of celebration and preparation for Scorpio. By focusing on meaningful connections, disciplined planning, and self-care, you'll close the year on a high note and set the stage for a fulfilling 2026.

Good Luck For 2025

www.ingramcontent.com/pod-product-compliance
Lightning Source LLC
Chambersburg PA
CBHW031501130726
47989CB00003B/1487